SCIENCE HIGHLIGHTS

Prehistory–A.D. 500

ANCIENT SCIENCE

By Charlie Samuels

Gareth Stevens
Publishing

Please visit our Web site www.garethstevens.com. For a free color catalog of all our high-quality books, call toll free 1-800-542-2595 or fax 1-877-542-2596.

Library of Congress Cataloging-in-Publication Data
Samuels, Charlie, 1961-
Ancient science : prehistory-A.D. 500 / Charlie Samuels.
    p. cm. — (Science highlights)
Includes index.
ISBN 978-1-4339-4136-8 (lib. bdg.)
ISBN 978-1-4339-4137-5 (pbk.)
ISBN 978-1-4339-4138-2 (6-pack)
1. Science, Ancient—Juvenile literature. I. Title.
Q124.95.S254 2011
509'.01—dc22

                         2010009083

Published in 2011 by
Gareth Stevens Publishing
111 East 14th Street, Suite 349
New York, NY 10003

© 2011 The Brown Reference Group Ltd.

For Gareth Stevens Publishing:
Art Direction: Haley Harasymiw
Editorial Direction: Kerri O'Donnell

For The Brown Reference Group Ltd:
Editorial Director: Lindsey Lowe
Managing Editor: Tim Cooke
Children's Publisher: Anne O'Daly
Design Manager: David Poole
Designer: Kim Browne
Picture Manager: Sophie Mortimer
Production Director: Alastair Gourlay

Picture Credits:
Front Cover: Shutterstock

Inside: iStockphoto: Tobias Helbig 36, Vladimir Piskunov 32tl, Maria Toutoudaki 21t; **Shutterstock:** Francisco Javier Ballester 11, Baloncici 32cr, Paul Banton 44t, W. H. Chow 22, Louise Cukrov 31, Idal 15cr, Images Talk 43cl, Janprchal 29, Doctor Kan 19cr, Jin Yang Lee 9, Pavle Marjanovic 10, Erick N 33, Mikhail Olykainen 6, Sang H. Park 18, Polartern 45, David H. Seymour 5, Aleksander Todorovic 20, Olga Utlyakova 30, Sybille Yates 19tl; **Thinkstock:** 7, 12, 13cl, 14, 16/17, 17cr, 21cr, 26, 27, 28, 34, 35tl, 35c, 37, 38, 39t, 40, 41, 42.

The Brown Reference Group has made every attempt to contact the copyright holders. If anyone has any information please contact info@brownreference.com

All Artworks Brown Reference Group

Manufactured in the United States of America
1 2 3 4 5 6 7 8 9 12 11 10

CPSIA compliance information: Batch #CS10GS: For further information contact Gareth Stevens, New York, New York at 1-800-542-2595.

Contents

Introduction

It is easy to see science as being very modern. In fact, the desire to understand the world and to develop technological improvements is as old as humankind.

The earliest humans learned to use stones as tools in order to make other tools or weapons from wood or bone. The domestication of plants and animals allowed people to settle in communities and grow crops, rather than moving around to hunt game or collect wild plants. Recorded history began with the invention of writing. People wrote down events; they also developed numbers to keep records of farm animals, grain, or trade. To keep track of the seasons, they devised calendars based on the study of the stars and the moon: astronomy.

The Classical Age

The first people we identify with science and whose names we know were Greek philosophers, such as Aristotle and Archimedes. They applied a systematic approach to collecting knowledge. The Greeks were also highly practical, and applied their knowledge to architecture. The same process was continued by the Romans, who built great aqueducts for water supply and thousands of miles of roads.

About This Book

This book focuses on the development of science and technology from the earliest period of human history through the classical age of ancient Greece and Rome to about A.D. 500. It contains two different types of timelines. Along the bottom of each page is a timeline that covers the whole period. It lists key events and developments, color-coded by category. Most of the 10 chapters also have a specific timeline, running vertically down the sides of the pages. This timeline provides more specific details about the particular subject of the chapter. Because of the lack of written records for much of the period covered by this book, most of the dates are estimates.

The Greeks applied systematic knowledge to practical skills such as architecture. The Parthenon in Athens was built to give the appearance of perfect proportion: the columns actually taper toward the top. ↓↓

Invention of the Wheel

The wheel has been reinvented several times. It first appeared at least 5,000 years ago, but opinion is divided on how the original invention might have happened.

➤ Inspiration for the vehicular wheel may have come from the potter's wheel.

TIMELINE
1,000,000 – 40,000 B.C.

750,000 B.C.
Homo erectus in France learns how to use fire.

1,000,000   800,000   500,000

KEY:

 Life Sciences

Technology

1,000,000 B.C. Human ancestors (*Homo erectus*) use hammers made from antlers to create other tools for cutting, drilling, and shaping.

500,000 Early *Homo sapiens* in Europe use wooden spears with five hardened points, designed to lodge in an animal's flesh.

Six thousand years ago, humans were already using drag technology such as plows and sledges. In parts of the world, heavy objects such as rocks and boats were moved using log rollers. As the object moved forward, rollers were taken from behind and replaced in front.

Possible Evolution of the Wheel

At some point it seems likely that someone combined the use of a sledge with the rolling logs. Eventually the sledge would settle into the worn section of the rollers, and maybe this gave people the idea of the axle wheel.

But there are problems with the roller theory—logs split quite easily when rolled under pressure, and tall, straight trees were not abundant in the Middle East, where the first solid evidence for transportation wheels appears.

The development of a wheel that rotates on a fixed axle is used by archaeologists as an indicator of relatively advanced civilization. The earliest evidence of axled wheels dates back to about 3200 B.C. The Sumerian people of Mesopotamia (modern-day Iraq) produced pictures of carts with solid wheels, with axles through the center. Similar wheels appeared on war

Timeline

3500 B.C. The first potters' wheels appear in Mesopotamia

3200 B.C. The first axled vehicular wheel appears (also in Mesopotamia)

2800 B.C. The Chinese develop the wheel

2000 B.C. The Sumerians develop the spoked wheel

85 B.C. The waterwheel is developed in Greece

A.D. 100 The Chinese invent the wheelbarrow

A.D. 500–1000 The spinning wheel is developed in China

⬅ The wheel is one of the most adaptable inventions. It led to the development of cogs, gears, engine flywheels—and spinning wheels.

150,000 European toolmakers insert a row of sharp flints into grooved pieces of wood or bone to make knives.

45,000 People in Europe make stone-headed spears and flint knives.

250,000   100,000   40,000

250,000 Early *Homo sapiens* in Africa, Asia, and Europe begin using stone axes.

80,000 In Mesopotamia and Europe, people make stone lamps that burn oil or candle fat.

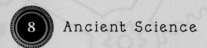

The Supernatural Wheel

There is no evidence that the wheel was used in ancient America. However, a hoard of what seem to be wheeled toys was carved in stone in Mexico in about 1500 B.C. So if the Aztecs knew how to make wheels, why didn't they ever use them? One theory is that the "toys" are, in fact, religious artifacts and that the wheel was seen as holy—it was reserved for the use of the Aztec gods alone.

⟶》 The Sumerians developed wheeled chariots, followed by the ancient Egyptians.

chariots built by the Sumerians in about 2500 B.C. About 500 years later, the Sumerians developed spoked wheels, which made chariots lighter and more maneuverable. Over the next 500 years, the design spread and was refined by other civilizations, including the Egyptians and the Romans.

Different civilizations may have come up with the wheel independently. In China, for example, the wheel appeared in about 2800 B.C.

Other Kinds of Wheels

The first wheels were probably not intended for transportation. Evidence from around 3500 B.C. shows that potters were using simple turntables to help them create smooth pots.

These early potters' wheels were developed further by the Greeks and Egyptians into flywheels that could convert pulses of energy, such as the pressing of a treadle, into smooth, continuous motion. The

↓⌄ Stone "toys" show that the Aztecs understood the idea of the wheel.

TIMELINE
40,000 – 10,000 B.C.

30,000 B.C. Europeans use tally sticks, or notched pieces of bone, for counting.

40,000   35,000   30,000

KEY:

Life Sciences

Technology

38,000 B.C. In Africa, people use a hook and line to catch fish.

25,000 People in central Europe fire clay models to make ceramic images; they do not yet make clay pots.

flywheel was to become just as important as the vehicular wheel. The Greeks also came up with other crucial mechanical variations on the wheel. The fourth and third centuries B.C. saw the development of cogs, gearwheels, and pulleys. The waterwheel was another important variation. Developed around 85 B.C., waterwheels allowed humans to harness the power of water to drive heavy machinery, namely millstones for grinding grain.

Since ancient times there have been several more wheel innovations. The Chinese began using spinning wheels for manufacturing yarn between A.D. 500 and 1000; the development reached Europe early in the 13th century. The spinning wheel is a variation on the flywheel: as the wheel turns, it rotates a spindle that twists fibers together to make thread many times faster than can be done by hand.

The flywheel was crucial to the Industrial Revolution. When connected to pistons driven by a steam engine, it converted pulses of raw power into smooth movement that could be used to drive machines or to power locomotives. Later still came wheel-based innovations including turbines, gyroscopes, and castor wheels—all variations on an ancient technology that is still going strong today.

↑ This ancient waterwheel still functions today, lifting water to supply neighboring fields.

20,000 In France, Cro-Magnon people produce stone blades shaped like leaves.

11,000 Mediterranean people fish using nets.

11,000 Hunter–gatherers in northern Syria begin to cultivate rye.

20,000

15,000

10,000

20,000 Europeans invent new hunting weapons, including the boomerang (made from mammoth tusk) and the wooden bow and arrow.

15,000 Africans use stone harpoons to spear fish.

11,000 The earliest known clay pots are made in Japan.

Writing and Numbers

Early writing took the form of symbols that signified exactly what they represented; they slowly acquired more abstract meanings, and eventually developed into writing.

→» Egyptian hieroglyphs began as representations of objects, but later could stand for sounds as well as objects.

TIMELINE
10,000–
5000 B.C.

KEY:

Life Sciences

Technology

10,000 B.C. People in Palestine make houses from sun-dried bricks and weave baskets.

9000 In Palestine, farmers cultivate einkorn wheat; emmer wheat is grown in present-day Turkey.

8000 Goats and sheep are domesticated in East Africa and Mesopotamia.

10,000

9000

8000

10,000 B.C. Dogs are domesticated in Mesopotamia (now Iraq), probably as food but later as pets.

8500 Native peoples in North America make stone arrowheads.

8000 In Central America, people cultivate pumpkins and squashes.

Writing developed as a way of keeping records. It began with simple drawings: "Sun" might be a circle inside a larger circle, and "water" might be depicted as a wavy line. In time, such signs came to have more than one meaning. The sign for "Sun" also meant "day," or in Egypt the sun god Re (or Ra).

In the next stage each sign came to represent a sound as well as an object, or simply a sound. This type of writing, in which pictures represent sounds, is called "hieroglyphics." (Each picture is known as a "hieroglyph.") The best-known type was developed in Egypt, where it first appeared around 3100 B.C.

At about the same time another system of writing was emerging in Mesopotamia, in present-day Iraq. It also began as a system of stylized pictures, but it developed very differently from hieroglyphics, because of the tools used to write it. Egyptian scribes wrote on papyrus paper with pens and ink, but Mesopotamian scribes pressed a writing tool called a stylus into soft clay, making a wedge or round shape. This type of writing is called cuneiform. It came into use in about 2400 B.C. and was used by the Sumerians, Assyrians, and Babylonians. It also spread to Persia and remained in use for nearly 2,000 years.

The first real alphabet (the Proto Canaanite) emerged in the Middle East

Timeline

3400 B.C. Numbers (base 10) used in Egypt

3100 B.C. Egyptian hieroglyphs

2400 B.C. Cuneiform writing

1700 B.C. Early Chinese writing

1700 B.C. Proto-Canaanite alphabet

1000 B.C. Phoenician alphabet

→→ Sumerian cuneiform was pressed into clay using a wedged-shaped stylus.

7000 In Asia Minor (present-day Turkey), pigs are domesticated for meat and leather.

6500 The Chinese, who have gathered wild rice for centuries, cultivate rice in the Yangtze delta.

5000 People in Italy make the first mirrors, from obsidian.

7000   6000   5000

7500 The Mesopotamians use clay tokens for record keeping.

6500 Cattle are domesticated in Africa and Asia.

6300 Found in the Netherlands, the earliest dug-out boat was hollowed from a tree trunk about this time.

Babylonian Math Lives

The math we use today is to base 10, and the value of a digit depends on its position. So, 87 is 8 "tens" plus 7 "units." The Babylonians used base 60. They would have written 87 as 1 "sixty" plus 27, or 1 27. It is similar to the way we might write 87 minutes as 1 hour 27 minutes. This is no coincidence. We still use the Babylonian base 60 system for time (hours, minutes, and seconds) and for geometry (degrees, minutes, and seconds). There are 360 degrees (six "sixties") in a circle.

in about 1700 B.C. It used 30 symbols to represent single sounds. From this, the Phoenician alphabet of 22 letters developed by about 1000 B.C., later giving rise to Arabic, Hebrew, Latin, and Greek scripts.

Chinese writing also developed from pictures. The symbols were in use from about 1700 B.C. They became more abstract during the Zhou Dynasty (c.1122–256 B.C.).

↑ Hieroglyphs were slow to write, so Egyptians developed an easier, quicker script.

Counting Numbers

Record keepers also needed a way to write numbers. A picture of one cow can represent one cow, but it would be impractical to show 60 cows by drawing each one. In about 30,000 B.C. in what is now the Czech Republic, someone carved 11 groups of five notches on a bone. It is clearly a numerical record. A stick or bone used in this way is called a tally stick.

TIMELINE
5000–4000 B.C.

5000 B.C. In Mesopotamia, people use rod-shaped distaffs to spin yarn from wool.

4500 Central Americans cultivate avocados for food and cotton for yarn.

5000   4800   4600

KEY:

Life Sciences

Technology

5000 B.C. Arable farming begins in Mexico and Central America, where farmers grow corn (maize).

5000 Egyptians smelt copper from its ore and use it to make weapons and other implements.

Numerals greater than 10 were first used in Egypt in about 3400 B.C. and in Mesopotamia in about 3000 B.C. Most cultures used ten as a base, probably because humans have ten fingers. The Babylonians and Sumerians were exceptions: they calculated to base 60.

Egyptian and cuneiform numbers used different symbols for 1; 10; 100; 1,000; 10,000; 100,000; and 1,000,000, and indicated higher values by repeating them, as in Roman numerals, where X is 10, XX is 20, and XXX is 30; C is 100, and CCC is 300. However, none of these systems had a symbol for zero.

Thousands of cuneiform tablets have survived. Some were used by students to learn multiplication tables and complex calculations. Egyptians, on the other hand, used only addition and the two times table. They multiplied by repeatedly doubling or halving and then adding the results.

Proto Canaanite	Early letter names and meanings	Phoenician	Early Greek	Early monumental Latin	Modern English
	alp oxhead				A
	bêt house			B	B
	gaml throwstick				C
	digg fish			D	D
	hô(?) man calling				E
	wô mace				F
	zê(n) ?				
	hê(t) fence?			H	H
	tê(t) spindle?				
	yad arm				I
	kapp palm			K	K
	lamd ox-goad				L
	mêm water			M	M
	nahs snake				N
	cên eye				O
	pi't corner?				P
	sa(d) plant				
	qu(p) ?				Q
	ra's head of man			R	R
	taan composite bow				S
	tô owner's mark			T	T

↑ Most of the letters in our modern English alphabet can be traced back to the Phoenician alphabet, as shown here. However, the Phoenicians made no distinction between the letter J and the letter I.

↑ Roman letters often had straight lines so they were easy to carve in stone.

VIRGINI·SEMPER·IMMACVLATAE

4300 In France, people make oak canoes up to 16 feet (5 m) long.

4000 The horse is domesticated in Ukraine, initially as food and later as a beast of burden.

4000 The first lock is invented in Mesopotamia.

4400　4200　4000

4400 Egyptians use linen made from wild flax to weave cloth on a loom.

4236 The ancient Egyptians introduce a 365-day calendar.

4000 Builders in Egypt and Mesopotamia learn to construct arches.

Agriculture and Food

About 11,000 years ago, people began to give up the hunter-gatherer way of life and live in settlements where they could grow crops and rear animals.

← This Egyptian tomb painting shows a farmer using an ox to pull a plow.

TIMELINE
4000– 3000 B.C.

KEY:

Life Sciences

Technology

4000 B.C. Potatoes are domesticated as a crop in the highlands of the Andes.

4000 The Egyptians use donkeys as beasts of burden.

3500 Farmers in China and Mesopotamia use the first plows.

4000   3800   3600

4000 B.C. In what is now Turkistan, people begin growing grapes vines to make wine.

3500 The wheel is invented in Mesopotamia, originally as a potter's wheel.

→> In some regions of the world, fields are still tilled as they were in ancient times, by oxen pulling simple wooden plows.

I n the fertile valley of the Nile River in Egypt and in Mesopotamia between the Tigris and Euphrates rivers (in present-day Iraq), early farmers used digging sticks and hoes to prepare the soil for planting and sickles to harvest crops. The plow, invented in about 3500 B.C. in Mesopotamia and China, greatly extended the areas of land that could be tilled to grow food. Over the years, selective breeding resulted in higher-yielding strains of cereal plants such as wheat and barley. People also applied domestication and

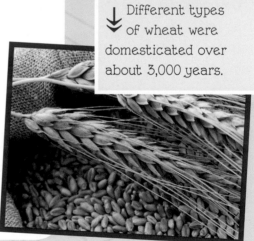

↓ Different types of wheat were domesticated over about 3,000 years.

3200 The Egyptians build nilometers to measure the height of the Nile and predict the annual flood.

3200 The first wheeled vehicles are used in western Asia.

3000 People settle in the Aegean region of Greece.

3400

3200

3000

3400 The Sumerians of Mesopotamia use a simple form of picture writing.

3200 Bronze, an alloy of copper and tin, is first used in Mesopotamia: it spreads through the Middle East and Europe.

3100 Egyptians begin using hieroglyphs as a form of writing.

Crops in the New World

Cereal crops were the first to be cultivated. Barley and wheat were probably first, then rice and corn (maize). Next, between 8,000 and 5,000 years ago, came root crops and legumes, such as beets and beans. Later still were fruiting trees, leafy vegetables, and crops grown to feed livestock. By 2,000 years ago, crops such as medicinal and cooking herbs were under cultivation. Some plants even began to be grown for their decorative value.

➤➤ Farming was painted in Egyptian tombs to ensure that the dead person had enough to eat in the afterlife.

selective breeding to animals. Beasts of burden, such as horses, oxen, and buffalo, began to replace human muscle power to carry loads, draw plows, and pull carts.

Storing and Processing Food

It was difficult to keep food over the winter, although people did store dried grain. Pulses (edible seeds), such as lentils and beans, could also be dried. Farmers killed many of their animals in late fall because they had

TIMELINE
3000–2500 B.C.

3000 B.C. The Mediterranean island of Cyprus becomes the ancient world's major source of copper.

2900 People in the Indus Valley in India cultivate cotton and spin its fibers into yarn.

2800 The Sumerians make soap from animal fat and plant ashes.

3000

2900

2800

KEY:

Life Sciences

Technology

3000 B.C. The first pottery in the Americas is made in Ecuador and Colombia.

2800 The Egyptians use fibers from reeds to make papyrus, an early form of paper.

insufficient food for them over the winter. People preserved animal carcasses simply by allowing them to dry in the wind, and in cold climates stored them in caves. New technologies arose from the need to store and preserve food. One method involved smoking meat or fish over a fire, a method still used today. Fish and meat were also salted. Curing (smoking) and salting of pig meat (pork) created ham and bacon.

People also began to use grindstones to make flour from harvested grains and to make clay pots to store food as well as for cooking. The earliest known pottery dates from about 11,000 B.C. in Japan. It was invented independently in the Middle East about 5,000 years later. As the potters grew more skillful, they built ovens for baking the clay.

↓ An 18th-century print shows harvesting with sickles, first used in ancient Egypt.

2700 In China, silkworms are raised on mulberry leaves; their cocoons are unwound to make silk.

2600 People in Mesopotamia make glass by melting silica (sand) and soda.

2500 In Egypt, physicians begin to practice surgery and develop medical instruments.

2700 2600 2500

2750 Mesopotamian builders use corbeled arches to build arches and domes.

2630 Work begins on the step pyramid of King Djoser, the first pyramid in Egypt.

2550 The Great Pyramid of King Khufu (Cheops) is completed at Giza in Egypt.

Ancient Medicine

Throughout history, doctors have healed the sick. In the ancient world, however, medical understanding of how the body worked was relatively limited.

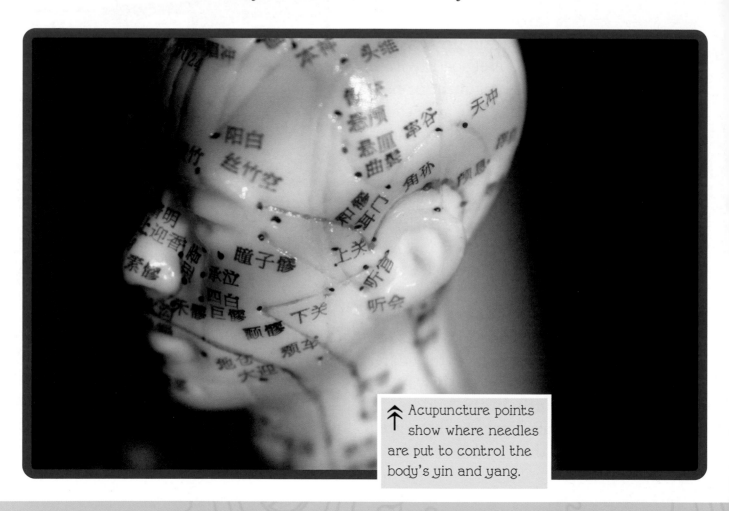

↑ Acupuncture points show where needles are put to control the body's yin and yang.

TIMELINE 2500–2000 B.C.

2500 B.C. Clay water pipes are used at Knossos in Crete and Mohenjo-Daro in what is now Pakistan.

2400 Mesopotamians invent the umbrella or parasol.

2300 Babylonian astronomers study constellations and other heavenly phenomena.

2500

2400

2300

KEY:

Life Sciences

Technology

2500 B.C. Sumerian traders introduce a standard system of weights and measures.

2400 The Egyptians domesticate cats: they see some cats as sacred and make them into mummies.

2300 Work begins on stone circles at Stonehenge in England, already an ancient ceremonial center.

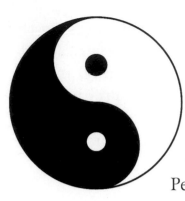

People who had not yet learned how the human body functions believed there were two classes of illness. Trivial complaints, such as an upset stomach, headache, or cold, were part of everyday life. People put up with them and treated them with whatever remedy seemed to work.

More serious illnesses, such as fevers or dysentery, were the work of demons or of gods who had been offended. They avenged themselves by throwing darts or worms into the victim's body or by extracting some important part—often the soul. Treatment involved removing the dart, worm, or demon causing the symptoms or encouraging the soul to return to its proper place. Practitioners would use suction or manipulation of the patient's body as well as administer herbal medicines and perform incantations. Treatment therefore involved magic or religious ritual, and those who performed it were known as "medicine men" or "medicine women."

↑ A Chinese symbol shows a perfect balance between yin and yang.

↑ Some ancient skulls have holes made in them, probably to release the evil spirits believed to cause mental illnesses.

Timeline

2500 B.C. Imhotep becomes the Egyptian god of medicine

2500 B.C. Acupuncture is practiced in China

1790 B.C. Hammurabi, king of Babylon, lays down laws to punish doctors for mistakes

1200 B.C. Asclepius, the Greek god of medicine, may have flourished around this time

2100 The Sumerians build a ziggurat (temple) of mud-baked bricks at Ur.

2000 In Syria and Babylon, doctors practice medicine based on astrology.

2200

2100

2000

2200 Iron is used for weapons in what is now Turkey.

2000 People in Peru domesticate guinea pigs for food.

2000 Chinese emperors keep animals in one of the first zoos, called the Park of Intelligence.

Greek God of Healing

In Greek mythology, Asclepius was raised by a centaur who taught him healing, and the Greeks worshipped him as the god of healing. Hundreds of temples to Asclepius were built across Greece. Sick people slept at the temples and were visited by Asclepius in a dream. The next day they told their dreams to priests, who gave them advice about what was needed to cure them.

→ Ayurvedic yoga is still practiced today, as a healthy exercise and also as part of Hinduism.

Drilling a hole 1 to 2 inches (2.5 to 5 cm) across in the top of the skull was one way to allow whatever caused an illness to escape. This was called trepanning, and it was practiced in many parts of the world. Prehistoric trepanned skulls have been found in Europe and also in Peru. The patient often survived the treatment. In the ancient skulls, bone has regrown to seal the holes.

China and India

Chinese medicine began over 4,500 years ago. Chinese doctors believed that illness was caused by imbalances between the female (yin) and male (yang) cosmic principles, and their treatment aimed to correct the imbalance. Doctors used herbal remedies, including ginseng.

Acupuncture was first

TIMELINE
2000–1500 B.C.

1950 B.C. In Palestine, farmers make plows with iron blades.

1800 Mathematicians in Mesopotamia discover what is now known as the Pythagorean Theorem.

2000   1900   1800

KEY:

Life Sciences

Technology

2000 B.C. Spoked wheels are used on chariots in Egypt and the Middle East.

1900 In Persia (now Iran), farmers cultivate alfalfa as a fodder crop for animals.

1750 In Babylon, King Hammurabi asks astronomers to compile catalogs of stars and planets.

← This Greek carving shows a doctor treating a patient.

↓ The Greek physician Hippocrates of Cos, after whom the doctors' Hippocratic oath is named, is seen as the father of medicine.

practiced more than 4,500 years ago. Chinese scientists believed the body contained three "burning spaces" and that the cosmic principles (yin and yang) circulate through 12 channels. Acupuncture aims to alter the distribution of yin and yang in the channels and burning spaces. The technique involves inserting warm or cold metal needles into the skin at particular points on the body that are related to particular organs. There are hundreds of such points.

Ayurvedic medicine, based on religious writings called the "Vedas," is still used in India, where it began about 3,000 years ago. The aim is to prevent illness through lifestyle, hygiene, and yoga, and to cure complaints by using herbal and mineral preparations and the correct diet. Ayurvedic practitioners treat the whole person rather than simply dealing with a particular illness.

1600 Astrologers in Babylon recognize the zodiac, the path of the sun, moon, and planets through the sky.

1500 On Crete, the Palace of Minos has bathrooms with running water.

1500 In Mexico, people make toys with wheels—but do not yet use wheels for transportation.

1700   1600   1500

1700 People in Syria develop a phonetic alphabet with 30 symbols, each representing a sound.

1600 Bellows are used in Mediterranean countries to increase the heat of fires for metalworking and glassworking.

1500 On the Gulf Coast of Central America, the Olmec culture builds complexes of pyramids and temples.

The Pyramids

The Great Pyramid at Giza is still standing after 4,500 years. That shows the technological skill and ingenuity of the ancient civilization that built it.

➤➤ The Great Pyramid rises behind the Sphinx, a statue of a lion with a man's head.

TIMELINE
1500–
1000 B.C.

1500 B.C. The Mitani of what is now Armenia learn to smelt iron from its ore: the technique passes to the Hittites.

1400 Stonehenge is completed in southern England.

1361 Chinese astronomers record the first known solar eclipse.

1500

1400

1300

1500 B.C. The Egyptians use the shaduf—a bucket on a long lever—to raise water from rivers for irrigation.

1450 The Egyptians use a water clock (clepsydra) to tell the time.

1350 Egyptians and Hittites begin working with iron.

KEY:

 Astronomy and Math

Life Sciences

Engineering and Invention

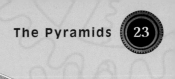

Humankind seems compelled to create tall buildings. Four thousand years ago, the only shape for such a structure was a broad base tapering at the top. Smooth-sided pyramids seem to have been a progression from the ziggurats built in Mesopotamia and Persia between 3000 and 500 B.C. A ziggurat was a temple-tower built in several levels, each smaller than the one below. It may have represented a sacred mountain or a link between Earth and heaven. Ziggurats had from two to seven tiers, built of mud.

Pyramids in Egypt

The first pyramid in Egypt was built at Saqqara in about 2630 B.C. It had a stepped structure, but was made of stone rather than mud. Within 30 years, the Egyptians had refined the design and were building smooth pyramids, such as the Red Pyramid at Dahshur, seen as the first "true" pyramid. The massive blocks at the core were cased in smaller blocks to smooth the outline.

The pyramids were burial structures built to honor the kings (or pharaohs), who were seen as living gods.

↑ The ziggurat at Ur was built around 2100 B.C. using sun-baked mud bricks.

Timeline

2630 B.C. First pyramid built in Egypt at Saqqara

2600 B.C. First true pyramid built, the Red Pyramid at Dahshur

2550 B.C. Great Pyramid at Giza completed

2250 B.C. Last pyramid built in Egypt, for Pharaoh Pepi II at Saqqara

---

1150 Chinese workers cast bells from bronze.

1050 Invaders from Anatolia introduce ironworking to Greece.

1000 The kite is invented in China; it is probably the first heavier-than-air flying object.

1200

1100

1000

1200 Coastal fishermen in Peru make rafts and boats from reeds.

1100 In China, craftsmen use spinning to produce yarn from cotton and wool.

1000 Chinese scribes write on bamboo or tree bark using brushes and black ink made from ashes and tree gum.

Which Ramps?

The ramps used by the pyramid builders are the subject of much speculation. The simplest ramps approached one side of the pyramid. But to maintain a shallow gradient, they would have to have been very long and contain almost as much building material as the pyramid itself. Other ramp designs, such as zigzags and spirals, would have used less material but would be more complex structurally.

Detailed plans were drawn up by skilled draftsmen working on sheets of papyrus. Sometimes the pyramids were built over natural features such as rocky outcrops. This meant that fewer materials had to be imported but made surveying and measuring more difficult.

Engineering the Pyramids

Egyptian pyramids are built along a precise north–south axis. The Egyptians used a surveying tool called a bay to determine true north from the stars. The pyramids show that the Egyptians also knew geometry. Anything less than a perfect square at the base would

↓ Zigzag and spiral ramps, and a side-on ramp (right), shown growing with a pyramid.

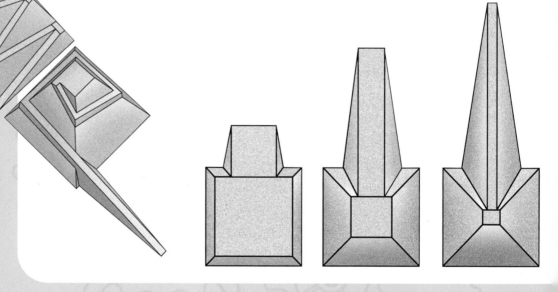

TIMELINE
1000–
800 B.C.

1000 B.C. The Phoenicians of the eastern Mediterranean introduce a 22-letter alphabet.

950 Farmers in northern and central Europe grow oats, which are better suited to the cool climate than wheat.

1000   975   950   925

1000 B.C. In Italy, Etruscan craftsmen use gold to make false teeth.

980 A Chinese writer recommends using steam to sterilize objects.

950 The Phoenicians make purple dye from the Murex sea mollusk: it is so rare and expensive, only rulers are allowed to wear clothes dyed with it.

KEY:

Astronomy and Math

Life Sciences

Engineering and Invention

mean that the four sides would fail to form a neat point at the apex at the top. The same perfection was required of the stone blocks, which were shaped by skilled masons.

The real secret of the pyramids may lie in the use of a vast workforce. Estimates of the numbers involved vary from 100,000 to just a few thousand. In general, the estimates have fallen as our knowledge has increased. It is unlikely that these people were slaves. There is archaeological evidence of communities centered on the construction sites, providing accommodation and services for a huge, highly specialized workforce.

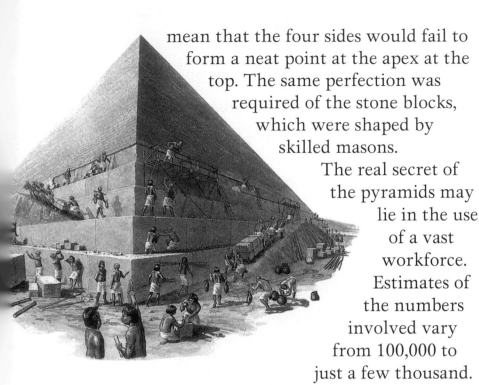

↑ The pyramids were made from huge blocks of stone with an outer casing of smaller blocks.

Moving the Blocks

The stone blocks for the pyramids weighed many tons. They were quarried as nearby as possible or brought by boat along the Nile River. To carry the stone to the top of the pyramid, the builders used huge straight or zigzag ramps up which they could drag the blocks on wooden sleds. At the top, levers were used to maneuver the blocks into position.

↞ A diagram shows the complex structure of a pyramid, with chambers, access tunnels, and air vents.

900 In Mesopotamia, farmers use irrigation to get better harvests.

850 The first known stone arch bridge is built at Smyrna, now Izmir in Turkey.

875   850   825   800

900 The Chinese cast metal coins in the shape of shovels or knives.

850 The Chinese use natural gas—probably methane from underground deposits—for lighting, conveyed along "pipes" of bamboo.

800 Egyptians use artificially heated incubators to hatch eggs.

Using Metals

Egyptians were making copper tools and weapons around 7,000 years ago. As the technology spread, new, improved metals shaped the development of society.

→ The so-called Mask of Agamemnon was made from gold around 1500 B.C.

TIMELINE
800–600 B.C.

763 B.C. Babylonian astronomers record an eclipse of the sun.

750 The Greek poet Homer records the burning of sulfur to fumigate plants and kill pests.

800

750

725

700 B.C. Phoenicians build biremes—boats with two rows of oars on either side.

KEY:

Astronomy and Math

Life Sciences

Engineering and Invention

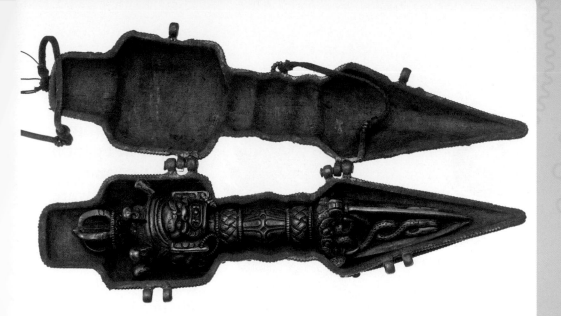

↑ Ancient daggers were often used as ritual objects rather than for practical purposes.

Timeline

c.5000 B.C. Egyptian weapons and tools made of copper

c.3200 B.C. Bronze produced throughout the Middle East

c.3000 B.C. Copper axes produced in the Balkans in southeastern Europe

c.2000 B.C. Iron produced by metalworkers in southern India

c.1600 B.C. Mycenaean daggers with bronze, gold, and silver

c.1400 B.C. Ironworking becomes important to the Hittites of Anatolia (Turkey)

1323 B.C. Egyptian king Tutankhamun is buried with a funeral mask made of gold inlaid with lapis lazuli

c.1000 B.C. Ironworking has spread across Europe

c.200 B.C. Early steel is produced in India

Some of the earliest metal artifacts are of gold and silver. In Egypt, the famous burial mask of Tutankhamun was made from gold. Gold and silver vessels, ceremonial weapons, and ornaments have been found in graves throughout the eastern Mediterranean and western Asia. On its own or alloyed with silver to make electrum, however, gold is too soft for making tools or weapons. Gold and silver were purely decorative.

The Copper Age

Copper was different. In order to use copper, the lumps of metal must be melted and then cast in molds. Hammering then hardens the copper, allowing it to be

600 In Central America, the Maya use pods from the cacao plant to make drinking chocolate.

675

625

600

691 King Sennacherib of Assyria builds a 50-mile (80-km) aqueduct to carry water to his capital, Nineveh.

600 The Greek artist Glaucus of Chios produces an alloy that melts easily and uses it to solder metals.

Rich Egyptians were buried with lavish jewelry made from precious metals.

used to make blades. Weapons and tools were made from copper in Egypt by 5000 B.C., and copper axes were being made in the Balkans by 3000 B.C. People also discovered that they produced more copper if they melted it in the presence of a particular blue stone. They had begun to extract a metal from its ore, in this case azurite.

The Bronze Age

Sometime after 4000 B.C., people began to mix tin with copper to form the alloy bronze. It is much harder than copper, and bronze tools stay sharper longer. Bronze was made in what is now southern Iraq between 3200 and 2500 B.C. It spread relatively quickly throughout the Middle East and Europe. As it did so, the Copper Age gave way to the Bronze Age.

TIMELINE
600–400 B.C.

560 B.C. The Greek philosopher Xenophanes of Colophon realizes that the presence of fossil seashells high on mountains means that the land was once below sea level.

535 The Greek physician Alcmaeon dissects animals to study their anatomy.

515 The philosopher Anaximander of Miletus introduces the sundial to Greece as a way of telling the time.

600

575

525

550 B.C. The Greek mathematician Pythagoras works out the relationship between the length of a vibrating string and the note it produces.

513 King Darius of Persia builds a 2,000-foot (610-m) floating bridge to allow his army to cross the Bosphorus to invade Greece.

KEY:

Astronomy and Math

Life Sciences

Engineering and Invention

The Coming of Iron

Iron is difficult to obtain from its ore because it has a very high melting point; the process also needs repeated melting and hammering. But iron was being produced in southern India around 2000 B.C. An iron dagger blade dating from about 2200 B.C. was found in Anatolia (now Turkey). Iron was important to the Hittites by 1400 B.C. and by 1000 B.C. had spread across Europe.

➤➤ A bronze helmet worn by a Greek soldier, with openings only for the eyes and mouth.

Iron is soft, so it could not compete with bronze. But smiths found that iron is strengthened if kept at bright-red heat in a charcoal fire. By absorbing carbon from the charcoal, iron is converted into steel, which is made stronger still if it is plunged into water while red hot. Steel was first made in India in about the third century B.C. Stories about swords with special powers probably refer to steel blades that were stronger than bronze.

Alloys

An alloy is a mixture of two or more metals, often with small amounts of other elements. Alloys are made by isolating the metallic ingredients, mixing the metals in the required proportions, and finally melting the metals together. The properties of an alloy differ from those of the metals that make it. The first alloys were of copper and tin, which make bronze. The finest bronze contains 89 percent copper and 10 percent tin, with very small amounts of other metals.

---

430 In four famous paradoxes, Zeno of Elea challenges the accepted ideas about time and space.

400 The Chinese use counting boards with bamboo rods to make calculations.

475

425

400

434 Anaxagoras of Iona suggests that the sun is a ball of hot rock.

424 In wars between city–states in Greece, attackers use flamethrowers made of tubes holding burning charcoal, sulfur, and tar.

400 Mayan mathematicians develop a number system using base 20.

Calendars

Around 35,000 years ago, Africans carved notches on bones to mark the passage of time. Similar "calendar sticks" were made until recently by Native Americans.

⬆ A carved Aztec calendar, showing periods of time around the image of a god.

TIMELINE
400–200 B.C.

400 B.C. Hippocrates of Kos, said to be the founder of the Hippocratic oath taken by doctors today, describes human anatomy and the causes of some diseases.

340 The Greek physician Praxagoras of Kos distinguishes between veins and arteries.

330 Greek philosopher Aristotle proposes that Earth is at the center of the universe and the planets, moon, sun, and stars orbit it.

400   375   350   325

399 B.C. Authorities in Syracuse order the development of new weapons, including a repeating arrow-firing catapult.

387 The Greek thinker Plato opens an academy in Athens for the pursuit of philosophy and scientific research.

350 Aristotle draws up a classification scheme for animals and plants.

KEY:

Astronomy and Math

Life Sciences

Engineering and Invention

The Egyptian calendar was developed to predict the annual Nile flood.

Another African calendar, the Ishango bone, dates from 25,000 years ago. It probably counts the days from new moon to new moon (lunar cycle), over a period of six months.

All early calendars were based on this lunar cycle, including the first annual calendar, developed by the Egyptians in about 4236 B.C. However, the lunar calendar failed to predict the seasonal flooding of the Nile River. Egyptian astronomers found that when the star Sirius was visible shortly before sunrise, the Nile flood followed a few days later. They devised a calendar based on a solar year and lunar months. It had three seasons, each of four months of 30 days, with an extra five days at the end of the year, making a year of 365 days. They also used a measurement of time longer than a year: the reign of a king.

It was the Egyptians who first divided the day into 24 units. The units were not of equal length, however.

Timeline

33,000 B.C. Lebombo bone carved in what is now Swaziland

23,000 B.C. Ishango bone carved in present-day Democractic Republic of Congo

4236 B.C. The full Egyptian lunar calendar appears

3000 B.C. Sumerian calendar of months of 30 days

2950 B.C. Chinese lunar calendar

1800 B.C. Sumerian lunar-year calendar

1700 B.C. Babylon adopts the Sumerian calendar from Nippur

1100 B.C. The Assyrians adopt the Babylonian calendar

1000 B.C. Hindu lunar calendar

---

300 Greek mathematician Euclid writes *Elements*, a book of geometrical theorems.

235 In Greece, Eratosthenes calculates the circumference of Earth.

200 In what is now Peru, the Nazca begin "drawing" huge outlines of plants and animals in the desert.

275   250   225   200

312 Romans build the Aqua Appia, the first aqueduct to bring water into Rome.

283 Greek engineers build the Pharos lighthouse at Alexandria, Egypt: it is one of the Seven Wonders of the Ancient World.

214 The main part of the Great Wall of China—some 1,400 miles (2,250 km) long—is completed.

Early astronomers based the first calendars on the regular movements of stars and other heavenly bodies.

There were 12 daytime units and 12 nighttime units, and their lengths changed with the seasons.

The Sumerian Calendar

By about 3000 B.C., the Sumerians of what is now southern Iraq had divided the year into 12 months of 30 days each. There were 12 periods in a day, and periods were divided into 30 parts. The Sumerians also invented other calendrical measurements. The Sumerian year began at the time of the barley harvest, but the financial year began about two months later, when the grain was sent to market. The commencement of the year was a time when the king made offerings to the gods. The Sumerian calendar was adopted by the Babylonians in the 18th century B.C. and later by the Assyrians.

→ The zodiac was developed by the Babylonians, based on the movement of stars.

TIMELINE
200–100 B.C.

165 B.C. Chinese astronomers record the existence of sunspots.

150 The Greek astronomer Hipparchus of Nicaea calculates the distance from Earth to the moon.

200   180   160

KEY:

Astronomy and Math

Life Sciences

Engineering and Invention

200 B.C. In South America, metalworkers use blowpipes to create the draft for furnaces to make alloys of gold and silver.

150 Greeks and Romans use a screw press to crush olives to extract olive oil.

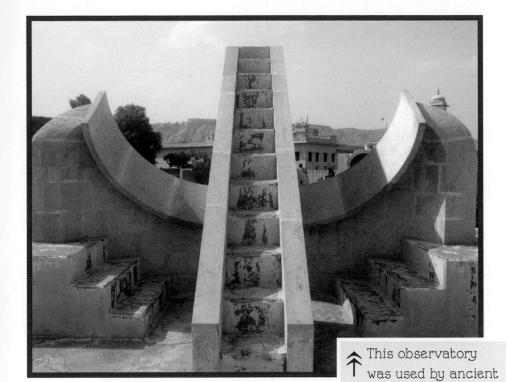

↑ This observatory was used by ancient Indian astronomers to study the heavens.

From about 2950 B.C., the Chinese developed a lunar calendar. It divides the year into 12 months of alternately 29 and 30 days, with additional months added from time to time to keep the calendar in step with the solar year.

The Hindu calendar, introduced around 1000 B.C., divides the year into 12 lunar months of 27 or 28 days, with an additional month inserted every five years. The year is also divided into three periods of four months. The start of each period is marked by a religious festival.

Months and Days

Some time before 2100 B.C., Sumerians began using lunar years. So, a loan made in a certain month could be repaid in the same month the next year. In about 1800 B.C., this produced a calendar of 12 months alternating between 29 and 30 days. The resulting year of 354 days— (29 x 6) + (30 x 6)— failed to coincide with the agricultural year as measured by the sun. So Sumerian cities inserted an extra month. The insertion was not standardized, so each city had its own calendar.

125 Chinese traveler Chang Ch'ien introduces wine grapes into China from the West.

100 Roman builders begin to use concrete made from crushed stones.

140

120

100

150 People in Ireland and Germany make roads by laying wooden planks together.

110 Roman horsemen begin to use nailed horseshoes.

100 Chinese mathematicians begin to use negative numbers.

Aristotle

Few individuals have influenced so many different areas of learning as Aristotle, who informed generations in areas such as logic, meteorology, physics, and theology.

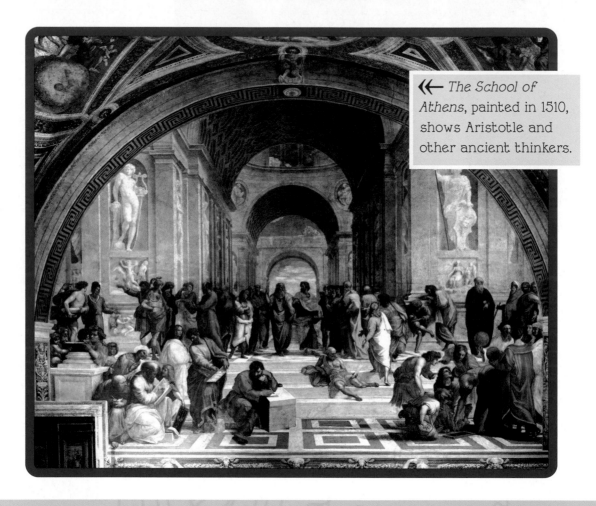

← *The School of Athens*, painted in 1510, shows Aristotle and other ancient thinkers.

TIMELINE
100 B.C.–0

KEY:

Astronomy and Math

Life Sciences

Engineering and Invention

100 B.C. The Romans develop a system for heating seawater to cultivate oysters.

75 The Greek physician Asclepiades of Bithynia asserts that disease is caused by discord in the body.

55 In India, the Hindu medical system called the Ayurveda becomes the basis of medical teaching.

100

80

60

80 B.C. Vertical waterwheels are used to grind corn in eastern Mediterranean regions.

52 A Chinese astronomer makes an armillary ring (used to represent the equator when observing stars).

Possibly the most influential thinker ever to have lived, Aristotle was born in 384 B.C. at Stagirus, a port in Macedonia. His studies took him to Athens to the Academy of the philosopher Plato (c.428–c.348 B.C.). He then spent several years traveling in Asia Minor and studying natural history.

In 342 B.C., the new king of Macedon, Philip, asked Aristotle to be a tutor to his 14-year-old son Alexander—the future Alexander the Great. After Philip was assassinated in 336 B.C., Aristotle returned to Athens. There, in 335 B.C., he established a school of his own, called the Lyceum. It was also called the Peripatetic School, because Aristotle was in the habit of lecturing while walking in the garden. After Alexander died in 323 B.C., Aristotle moved to Chalcis

⬆ A bust of Aristotle is a familiar sight in many places of high culture in the West.

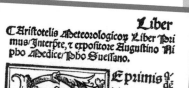

Timeline

384 B.C. Aristotle born at Stagirus

367 B.C. Studies at Plato's Academy in Athens

347 B.C. Leaves Athens

342 B.C. Becomes tutor to Alexander

336 B.C. Alexander becomes king; Aristotle returns to Athens

335 B.C. Aristotle founds the Lyceum

323 B.C. Alexander dies; Aristotle retreats to Chalcis

322 B.C. Aristotle dies

⬅ A page from a 16th-century book on Aristotle. His work was read for centuries after his death.

44 Astronomers in China and Italy report a red comet; the color is caused by ash from an explosion of a volcano.

30 Syrian craftsmen learn the technique of glassblowing, which is taken up by the Romans.

19 Roman general Marcus Agrippa orders the building of a 13-mile (21-km) aqueduct to bring water into Rome.

40

20

0

46 Emperor Julius Caesar introduces the Julian calendar.

28 Chinese astronomers begin keeping records of sunspots, which they continue until A.D.1638.

10 King Herod the Great of Judea uses concrete blocks to build an open harbor at Caesarea in Palestine.

Aristotle's Astronomy

Aristotle showed that Earth is round by observing that during a lunar eclipse, Earth casts a shadow with a curved edge onto the moon. He also observed that, while traveling north or south, new stars appear on one horizon while other stars disappear below the opposite horizon. This effect is visible over short distances, which suggested that Earth is not very large. Aristotle estimated the planet's diameter and came within 50 percent of the correct value.

(modern Khalkis) on the island of Euboea, his mother's birthplace. He died there in 322 B.C.

Aristotle's Teachings

Aristotle's teachings survive in works on philosophy, logic, politics, biology, physics, meteorology, and cosmology. They remained the basis of formal logic until the 19th century. His attempts to explain weather phenomena influenced the study of meteorology.

Aristotle was most successful as a biologist. He observed more than 500 animal species and classified them into hierarchies. He divided animals into those with blood and those without, approximately coinciding with the distinction we now make between vertebrates and invertebrates.

Animals that give birth to live young head Aristotle's

↓ Earth's shadow on the moon showed Aristotle that the planet was spherical.

A.D. 8 Horizontal waterwheels are used in China.

15 An Italian physician, Thaddeus of Florence, describes the uses of alcohol in medicine.

50 Greek mathematician Hero of Alexandria describes a simple steam turbine built as a novelty.

0

20

40

KEY:

Astronomy and Math

Life Sciences

Engineering and Invention

A.D. 1 Chinese mathematician Liu Hsin introduces decimal fractions.

30 Aulus Cornelius Celsus writes the first Latin treatise on medicine.

50 The Romans introduce Mediterranean vegetables to western Europe, including garlic and onions.

→ Aristotle realized that dolphins are more closely related to land animals than to fish.

Aristotle's View of Matter

Aristotle accepted the prevailing theory of his time that all matter is composed of the four elements: earth, air, water, and fire. But he added a fifth element, "aether," from which he believed that the heavens are made. Aristotle believed that Earth, and heaven were subject to different laws. On Earth, everything is corrupt, which means that it is changeable and liable to decay. The heavens, by contrast are permanent, unchanging, and perfect.

hierarchy, followed by those that lay eggs, those that produce eggs that hatch internally, those that lay eggs that are fertilized externally, those that reproduce by budding, and finally animals that arise spontaneously from slime or putrefying matter. From this arrangement, Aristotle compiled a "ladder of nature," which remained the basis of animal classification until it was overturned in the 18th century.

77 Roman scholar Pliny the Elder writes his 37-volume *Natural History*, summarizing Roman knowledge of the natural world.

80 The Colosseum is completed in Rome.

100 Chinese farmers introduce the tandem hitch, allowing two horses, one in front of the other, to pull plows and carts.

60   80   100

62 Hero of Alexandria writes *Metrica (Measurements)*, describing calculations of area and volume.

77 Greek physician Pedanius Dioscorides writes *De Materia Medica*, a catalog of drugs and herbs that remains authoritative for 1,700 years.

83 A Chinese writer describes an early form of compass, probably used for divination rather than navigation.

Archimedes

Archimedes is considered to be one of the greatest mathematicians of all time. His inventions brought him fame that lasts to this day.

→» Archimedes was said to have discovered one important theory while taking a bath.

TIMELINE
A.D. 100–200

KEY:

Astronomy and Math

Life Sciences

Engineering and Invention

105 A Chinese court official describes a way of making paper using tree bark, rags, and other materials.

110 In Greece, Menelaus of Alexandria introduces spherical geometry.

132 Chinese astronomer Zhang Heng builds a primitive planetarium to show the movement of important stars.

100

120

140

100 The wheelbarrow appears in China, where it is used to carry goods and people.

128 The Pantheon, a Greek-style temple, is built in Rome with a 142-foot (43-m) dome made of concrete.

140 Greek physician Aretaeus of Cappadocia describes many diseases and their treatment, including pleurisy and epilepsy.

An 1511 illustration shows Archimedes testing the purity of gold in a crown.

Archimedes (c.287–212 B.C.) was born in Syracuse, Sicily (then a Greek colony). He studied in Alexandria, Egypt, where his teacher was a former pupil of Greek mathematician Euclid. His studies completed, he returned to Syracuse, where he remained for the rest of his life.

Levers and Screws

Archimedes was the first to work out the principle underlying levers. He said that if he had somewhere to stand and a lever long and strong enough, he could move the world. King Hieron challenged Archimedes to move a very heavy object. Archimedes is said to have responded by assembling a system of levers and pulleys with which Hieron himself was able to pull the royal ship *Syracusa* across dry land.

Timeline

287 B.C. Archimedes born at Syracuse

270 B.C. King Hieron becomes king of Syracuse; he later asks Archimedes to discover whether his crown is pure gold

c.250 B.C. Archimedes screw pump

c.215 B.C. Romans lay siege to Syracuse; Archimedes designs weapons to defend the city

212 B.C. Siege of Syracuse ends; Archimedes killed by a Roman soldier

← An Archimedes screw pump is angled so that the tip of the tube is in the water. With each turn of the handle, water rises over each thread of the screw until it flows out of the tube's upper end.

175 Galen of Pergamum, a Greek physician, begins taking patients' pulse to aid diagnosis.

190 Chinese mathematicians express large numbers as powers of ten (e.g., 10^4 is 10 to the power 4, or 10,000).

160   180   200

150 The Greek geographer Ptolemy compiles *Almagest*, a digest of ancient knowledge of astronomy. It remains a standard work until the Renaissance, 1,300 years later.

185 Chinese astronomers observe a supernova (they call it a "guest star") in the constellation Centaurus.

He is said to have designed the screw pump to irrigate crops (the Egyptians may actually have had this much earlier). It is a spiral screw inside a cylinder that raises water. It is still used today.

Archimedes also helped defend Syracuse from a Roman siege in 215 B.C. The inventor came up with several novel weapons including the "claws of Archimedes," said to pick up and shake enemy ships, and a mirror that focused the sun's rays to set fire to enemy sails. Such weapons held the Romans at bay for three years.

↑ With the aid of various machines devised by Archimedes, including the fearsome "claws," the city of Syracuse held out against the Roman siege for three years.

Scientific Investigation

It is impossible to say whether Archimedes really built all the machines credited to him. He only published his mathematical work, and saw himself as primarily a

TIMELINE
A.D. 200–300

200 The Moche of coastal Peru build two huge terraced platform tombs from molded adobe brick, dedicated to the sun and the moon.

226 Built mainly on arches, the Aqua Alexandrina aqueduct carries water 14 miles (23 km) into Rome.

250 Greek mathematician Diophantus is credited with inventing algebra.

200   220   240

250 Parchment replaces papyrus as a writing material in the Mediterranean region.

KEY:

Astronomy and Math

Life Sciences

Engineering and Invention

→ Archimedes is said to have used a mirror to beam light on ships' sails to set them on fire.

mathematician. He calculated a value for pi that is very close to the modern figure, and devised methods for calculating the volume and surface area of a body with a curved surface. He also developed a way to express very large numbers, demonstrating it with a calculation of the number of grains of sand that exist in the universe.

The Romans took Syracuse in about 212 B.C. The general, Marcellus, ordered that Archimedes should not be harmed. A Roman soldier found Archimedes working on a mathematical problem and demanded that he accompany him. The mathematician told him not to disturb the circles he had drawn in the sand. Impatient, the soldier killed him.

269 The famous library at Alexandria is damaged when Queen Zenobia of Palmyra attacks Egypt.

300 The Romans notice that the British burn coal as fuel, and soon adopt the practice.

260   280   300

265 Chinese physician Huang Fu Mi writes a major treatise on acupuncture.

271 A compass is used in China for navigation; it is probably a piece of lodestone that indicates the direction of south.

Roman Roads and Aqueducts

From the fourth century B.C., the Romans built roads
throughout their sprawling empire, replacing mud tracks
with stone roadways on solid foundations.

→» The three-tiered
Pont du Gard was built
to carry water to the
French city of Nîmes.

TIMELINE
A.D. 300–
400

310 Chinese astronomer
Chen Zhuo combines the
maps of previous
astronomers into a single
comprehensive star map.

330 Chinese astronomer Yu Hsi
describes the precession of the
equinoxes, first discovered by
the Greeks in about 150 B.C.

350 An Indian account
of astronomy, the *Surya-
Siddhanta*, is published
at about this time.

300   320   340

302 A Chinese pottery
figure depicts a horseman
using metal stirrups.

350 The Chinese begin
to cultivate tea plants.

KEY:

Astronomy
and Math

Life Sciences

Engineering and
Invention

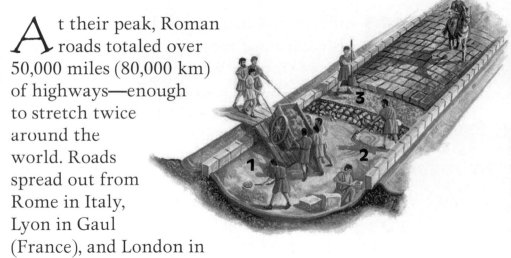

At their peak, Roman roads totaled over 50,000 miles (80,000 km) of highways—enough to stretch twice around the world. Roads spread out from Rome in Italy, Lyon in Gaul (France), and London in Britain. In North Africa, roads ran along the coast of the Mediterranean Sea.

The first Roman road was the Via Appia (Appian Way), built southward from Rome in 312 B.C. by Roman general Appius Claudius Caecus. Other roads soon followed, such as the Via Aurelia to Genua (Genoa) and the Via Flaminia to the Adriatic coast, each named after a different Roman dignitary. The Romans built roads mainly for

⟵ Parts of the Via Appia are still visible in Italy.

⟵ A construction crew works on the stages of road building, from clearing the roadbed (1) and building curbs (2) to laying stone courses as a foundation for the surface pavement (3).

Timeline

312 B.C. The Via Appia (Appian Way) is the first Roman road

C. 25 B.C. Vitruvius sums up Roman knowledge of engineering in his book *De Architectura (On Architecture)*

20 B.C. The Pont du Gard is built in France on the orders of the Roman general Marcus Agrippa

A.D. 80 The Colosseum is completed in Rome

A.D. 122 Construction begins on Hadrian's Wall in northern Britain

365 The first Western reference to mechanical cranks appears in a Greek text.

369 Chinese astronomers observe a supernova that remains bright for five months.

400 The Chinese begin to use the umbrella for protection from the sun and the rain.

360

380

400

350 Antioch (in what is now Turkey) becomes the first city to have a system of street lighting.

officials and merchants. But they were also useful for moving troops rapidly in case of trouble. Wherever possible, the roads followed a straight line set out by surveyors using a sighting staff called a groma. Fast chariots could achieve 75 miles (120 km) a day on the roads; freight wagons covered 15 miles (25 km) a day. As the Roman Empire crumbled, so did its roads owing to a lack of maintenance. Later road builders often took over the routes, as can be seen by the straight stretches on a road map of England.

↑ Hadrian's Wall was a 73.5-mile (118-km) long fortified barrier that helped control the northern frontier of Roman Britain.

⟫ A scaffold supported an arch while it was being built, with a central wedge-shaped keystone to lock the final structure in place.

Water for the Cities

As Roman towns and cities increased in size, there was an increasing demand for water for drinking and bathing: public baths and fountains were features of many Roman towns. To bring in the water, Roman engineers built aqueducts. An aqueduct is any permanent channel for carrying water.

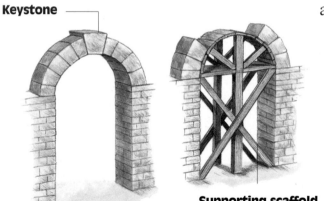

Keystone

Supporting scaffold

TIMELINE
A.D. 400–
500

400 Scholars in Alexandria use the Arabic term *al-kimiya* to describe changes in matter: it later gives rise to the words "alchemy" and "chemistry."

415 Indian engineers use iron chains to build suspension bridges.

400   420   440

KEY:

Astronomy and Math

Life Sciences

Engineering and Invention

405 Chinese craftsmen make steel by beating together wrought iron and cast iron.

410 The Greek mathematician Hypatia invents a hydroscope for measuring the density (specific gravity) of liquids.

↓ Rome's great amphitheater, the Colosseum, was completed in A.D. 80.

Between 312 B.C. and A.D. 200, engineers built a total of 11 aqueducts to carry water into Rome, some from over 56 miles (90 km) away. The aqueducts sloped very gradually—only a few inches in every mile—so that the water flowed along by gravity. Some Roman aqueducts in Italy, Greece, and Spain are still used today. They include the aqueduct at Segovia, Spain, which is made from 24,000 granite blocks fitted together without mortar in a series of 165 arches. The three-tiered arches of the famous Pont du Gard near Nîmes, France, extend for 900 feet (275 m) and reach a maximum height of 165 feet (50 m). It was built in about 20 B.C. by general Marcus Agrippa (63–12 B.C.). Both examples are still in full working order.

Stages of Road Building

Roman highway engineers first dug drainage ditches about 40 feet (12 m) apart, then cleared a trench between them, which they filled with sand, mortar, and a series of stone courses as the foundation. They topped the road with stone slabs or cobbles set in mortar. On marshy ground, the whole road was raised above the land. Some major roads had stone curbs 8 inches (20 cm) high and 2 feet (60 cm) wide on each side, with side lanes outside them.

489 Chinese artists carve 165-foot (50-m) statues of Buddha into a rock face at Yungang.

497 Indian mathematician and astronomer Aryabhata proposes that Earth rotates on its axis.

460

480

500

465 Chinese mathematician Tsu Ch'ung Chi uses a circle 3 meters across to calculate pi to 10 decimal places: 3.1415929203.

495 A Chinese writer describes a paddleboat with several paddle wheels along each side.

Glossary

alloy A blend of one metal with another to give it special qualities, such as resistance to corrosion or greater hardness. Common alloys include bronze, brass, and steel.

astronomy The study of objects outside Earth's atmosphere.

bronze A hard, durable alloy made mostly of copper and tin.

cuneiform The wedge-shaped writing used in Mesopotamia from the third to the late first millennium B.C.

distaff A rod on which yarn is wound.

domestication The use of selective breeding to adapt wild plants or animals to make them more useful to humans.

eclipse When two celestial bodies are lined up so that one blocks the light of the sun from the other.

hieroglyphics A system of writing, originating in ancient Egypt, that uses pictures to symbolize words.

hunter–gatherers People who follow a way of life based on hunting wild animals, fishing, and gathering berries, seeds, and wild food plants.

irrigation The watering of crops by artifical means, such as canals.

lodestone A mineral that is naturally magnetic.

lunar month The period from a full moon to a full moon.

ore A mineral from which a metal can be extracted.

papyrus A writing material used by the ancient Egyptians, made by beating together the stems of certain reeds.

philosopher A person who studies and tries to explain beliefs and concepts.

plow An agricultural implement that is pulled by an ox, horse, or modern tractor to cut, lift, and turn soil to prepare it for planting crops.

smelting Extracting metals from mineral ores by heating them to high temperatures.

solar year The length of time the sun takes to return to the same position in the cycle of seasons.

ziggurat A temple of rectangular tiers (larger at the base and smaller at the top) built with an outer covering of baked mud bricks.

Further Reading

Books

Asimov, Isaac, and Richard Hantula. *Astronomy in Ancient Times.* Gareth Stevens Publishing, 2005.

Burrell, R. *First Ancient History.* Oxford University Press, 1997.

Faiella, Graham. *The Technology of Mesopotamia.* Rosen Central, 2006.

Graham, Amy. *Astonishing Ancient World Scientists: Eight Great Brains.* Myreportlinks.com, 2009.

Gow, Mary. *Archimedes: Mathematical Genius of the Ancient World.* Enslow Publications, 2010.

Gow, Mary. *The Great Thinker: Aristotle and the Foundations of Science.* Enslow Publications, 2010.

Hightower, Paul. *The Greatest Mathematician: Archimedes and his Eureka! Moment.* Enslow Publications, 2009.

James, P., and N. Thorpe. *Ancient Inventions.* Michael O'Mara Books, 1999.

Landels, J.G. *Engineering in the Ancient World.* Constable, 2000.

Price, Joan A. *Ancient and Hellenistic Thought.* Chelsea House Publications, 2008.

Strap, James. *Science and Technology (Inside Ancient China).* Sharpe Focus, 2009.

Wiese, Jim, and Ed Shems. *Ancient Science.* Turtleback, 2003.

Zhu, Kang. *Science and Scientists: True Stories from Ancient China.* Long River Press, 2005.

Web Sites

http://www.mhs.ox.ac.uk
Web site of Oxford University's Museum of the History of Science.

http://ancienthistory.about.com/od/ sciencemedicine/Science_Math_ Medicine_Technology_Engineering. htm
About.com resource page with many links to pages about ancient science.

http://www.historyworld.net/wrldhis /PlainTextHistories.asp?historyid= aa32
The history of Greek science from History World.

http://www.swan.ac.uk/grst/
Swansea University Web site on Greek and Roman science and technology.

Index